Power Car Selling for the Inexperienced Salesperson

BRUCE BELLIS

CONTENTS

FORWARD

When mankind stopped using their feet as the major source of transportation, the salesperson was born. Whether it was horses, mules, camels, or later on, bicycles and motorized vehicles, the need for a buyer to purchase and the seller to sell has been fulfilled by a salesperson.

To be a salesperson doesn't require one to be a liar or a cheat. It does require effort on the person's part who would like to become a great retail automotive salesperson. It is a very rewarding career both in income and position. No longer can the old time car salespeople survive in this information rich society that has more makes and models to choose from than ever in history. To be successful it will take a commitment from you that you will strive to be better every day. Rewarding futures and careers start by being a retail automotive salesperson. There are many General Managers and Owners of dealerships today that started less than 15 years ago as a salesperson. It is also very common that to be promoted to a Sales or Finance Manager in a dealership you must have sales experience on the "floor" as a salesperson.

So what is this book about? It is about you and your future. I have spent 23 years in the retail automobile business and have decided to write this book in order to help the people who want to help themselves to a better income and future. The retail automobile business will always have a demand for good people and I want to prepare you for a successful and prosperous career as a retail automotive salesperson.

Why will this book be very important to you? It is because of the manner most dealerships hire new salespeople. The sad reality is that most dealerships run an employment ad to hire "green peas," (that is someone with no experience) hire them, hand them a brochure and maybe a product tape and set them out front to catch an "up." ("Up" is the word that is used to refer to customers) Unfortunately, thousands and thousands of salespeople hired by this manner only last a few months before leaving the retail automobile business. Unless the organization that you are working for has a fully committed training program and training manager, you will only survive by your developing your own skills. Managers tend to be cops rather than coaches. Most managers are too busy with their duties to slow down and train new salespeople. If an effort is made at training, the session usually ends up being interrupted so many times that nothing is really gained by it at all. There are very few managers that are helpful in the training process. You must take on the duty of training yourself every day. In this information rich society you can spend days researching make and models. Don't restrict product knowledge just to what you sell. You need to know about your competitor's makes and models in order to answer questions for your customers. Don't wait for others to help or train you!

Before going any further you might want to know if you're right for the car business. I can tell you that most people who go into the car business couldn't land a good paying job somewhere else. That's right. They finally submitted to the financial monkey on their back and answered that ad that talked about huge training salaries. Most hoped they could find a real job before the training salary ended. Then there are the individuals that see the full potential of the retail automotive business and they take advantage of it. They are the ones who know that they can do this car selling thing. They are the ones who are always learning, always listening, always trying to be better. It is an attitude, a drive, a belief in yourself.

No matter how many times you may read this book I can assure you that you will fail if you don't have the spirit to succeed. It will take a large effort to learn and retain everything this book has to offer you. If you want to have a distinct advantage over other "green peas" then you must follow this guide to help you be successful.

So, if you think that you have it in you to be a great car salesperson, let us continue and introduce you to the steps of a sale as well as the other daily duties that will help you be successful such as prospecting, asking for referrals, following up unsold customers and so much more. Each step of the sale will be explored, explained and dissected. Remember, it is your responsibility to learn and understand the material. The following is the list of the steps to a sale as I have used and taught.

1) PROMPT AND FRIENDLY GREETING
2) COMMON GROUND AND INFORMATION
3) SELECT A VEHICLE
4) STATIC PRESENTATION
5) DEMONSTRATION DRIVE
6) TRIAL CLOSE
7) TRADE APPRAISAL
8) WRITE UP
9) PRESENT THE ORDER
10) CLOSE
11) TURN OVER IF NEEDED
12) COMPLETION OF DEAL PAPERWORK
13) INTRODUCTION TO BUSINESS MANAGER
14) DELIVERY
15) FOLLOW-UP

There are two separate distinctions in the steps of a sale. One distinction is the "selling" and the other is "closing." Always remember that you cannot close what is not sold. In other words, if the customer isn't sold on you, a vehicle, and the dealership, they probably won't close on the sale. If you look at the steps to a sale, the first 8 steps are selling, and the rest are closing. Selling normally takes place outside on the lot while closing takes place inside the showroom. Generally, the more time you spend selling, the less time you will spend closing. The less time you spend closing leads to better commissions. I will explain that later in the closing steps.

You will need to be prepared with product knowledge of the vehicles you are selling prior to talking with a customer. Usually the manufacturer will provide the dealership with Salesperson's Product Knowledge Manuals and possibly DVD discs with product training information. Find these and start studying. You can never have too much product knowledge. The customer will often visit dealerships and the internet to find out the information about the vehicle they are interested in. They don't just look for pricing on the internet; they look for option packages, compatibility of options, colors and a vast amount of comparative information to other makes and models that they are also considering. When the customer engages into a conversation with you and it becomes obvious that you don't know your product, your chances of selling this customer just went down the drain. Over the years vehicles become more technologically advanced. Most of the manufacturers realized how important product knowledge training has become for sales and most offer Salespersons Certifications based on class room and internet training. If any training is offered, take as much of it as you can. You also can go on the internet and research the vehicles you are selling. This is a great way to understand what the consumers are looking at. The better understanding of the customer will always help close a sale.

We are not ready yet to talk to a customer. Ever hear "Dress for Success?" Take a look at yourself in a full mirror every day before you go to work. Do you look successful? Do you look neat and groomed? Do you look like you are confident? Have you paid attention to the details? Are your shoes shined? Let's get real. Looking sharp in business attire will give you an edge over other salespeople. Point in case, the customer you are talking to just departed from a dealership where the salesperson was not groomed, clothes were wrinkled and had shoes that should have been retired years ago. Do you think that the customers are even going to bother with product questions? They are more than likely to make a common objection and leave. Could this be the reason why they are at your lot and not buying a vehicle at the other? There could be a bunch of reasons why the customer hasn't bought yet and we will go through many of them just in the first step of a sale.

You only get one chance for a first impression and you better make it a good one.

The customers are always watching you to see how you react to them. When a customer arrives at a dealership they are hoping to meet a salesperson who is cheerful, friendly, and knowledgeable. The customer also hopes that the salesperson is not one of the high pressure types. What they are expecting is the direct opposite. When customers come into a dealership with what seems to be a chip on their shoulder it is in reality just fear. They are afraid of you, buying the wrong car, paying too much and losing respect from their family and friends. Many times the customers have devised a plan before coming to a dealership on how they will get in, find a vehicle, get a price and get out. They do this because of fear and your job is to make them feel comfortable with you and the dealership.

We still are not ready to talk to a customer yet. Even though we have acquired product knowledge and we are dressed accordingly, we need to complete a check up from the neck up before catching the next up. This business is mentally exhausting and challenging and you need to make sure you are in the right state of mind to talk to a customer. Walking out to a customer with a frown on your face is about the same as bringing a cold bucket of water to throw on them. Smile and the world smiles back. Always remember to smile when greeting a customer, they will smile back. A customer will not buy from somebody they dislike. Many deals are lost at the handshake because they way the salesperson greeted the customer. Something was said or a response to a question was mishandled by the salesperson. Whatever the reason, if a customer leaves the dealership within a few minutes of arrival, a potential sale has just been lost along with its commission because something went wrong. This is why I feel that the Prompt and Friendly Greeting step is the most important step.

1 PROMPT & FRIENDLY GREETING

We begin with a simple definition. Prompt means quick, Friendly means nice, and Greeting means to welcome and meet someone. Sounds simple doesn't it? Reality is this is where most of your potential sales blow up in smoke and you don't have a clue why. When a customer comes to a dealership they are usually nervous and cautious. They typically will have their "guard" up. You have probably heard from friends, family, and coworkers about the "nightmare" they had at a dealership. When approached by a salesperson the customer will often tell the salesperson that they are not buying and are just looking. Unfortunately the salesperson that believes that just got sold and closed. No Sale! No Commission! This is a standard objection that most customers use and there are a couple more that we will cover in this step.

Have you ever noticed that there is always some type of sale going on at every dealership? The reason for that is the fact that customers like sales. The customers always feel they are getting a better "deal" at a sale! If a customer has been inspired to drive on your dealership's lot, then you must assume they are there to buy a car and get a great "deal."

Now that we understand a little about what could be going on in the customers mind let me give you some word tracks to use in your greeting.

When approaching a customer walk briskly, but don't run at them. They are not meat and will more than likely leave if you and other salespeople are running at them. Remember to smile.

Ok, we are walking up to a customer. Here is the word track for the greeting.

"Hi, welcome to ABC Motors, are you here for our big sale?"

The reason I like this greeting is that it is simple and the only time you will hear "no" is when the customer is looking for service or parts or another department. If the customers came to look at vehicles, then you will get a "yes" or "what sale."

Never use "Can I help you?" as a greeting. You will almost all of the time get a "no, just looking" response. That is starting the sale in the basement and it will be tough to break the ice.

When the customer has given you a "yes" or "what sale" you need to know what current event sale is going on or what ad is running.

Here is the response word track.

"That's great; right now the dealership is having a (fill-in the blank) sale. As a matter of fact, we have already sold a bunch of cars and some at really good prices."

Here is where you start to establish control of the sale. By you controlling the conversation and directing the customer your success rate at closing will increase dramatically. Before the customer starts to ramble on or starts to blurt out common objections you will want to introduce yourself to your customers and give them your job description.

Here is the word track for the introduction.

**By the way, my name is (your name), and you are
_____, (introduce yourself to everybody
present. You don't know who the buyer and/or the
decision maker are at this point.) Very nice to meet
you, again my name is (your name) and my job as
a salesperson here at ABC Motors is to help you
find the vehicle that will fit all your needs,
wants, and desires and get you the very best
price possible. Is that fair?**

Of course you will get a "yes" in some form or
fashion. Remember that the customer is still in
defense mode and won't give many commitment
comments at this time, so anything other than a "no"
is a "yes." This is when the three standard common
objections you will hear most of the time will come
out. I have always told my salespeople that the
earlier these come up in the sale process the better it
is for us. Selling and closing are based on emotions.
The customers who have there "guard" up and are
nervous are thinking logically and not emotionally
and will try to put up some type of a defense system.
When the customer is thinking logically you have
very little chance of closing them on a sale. A great
selling job is when you have their logical thinking
down and their emotional thinking highly elevated.

FIRST STANDARD COMMON OBJECTION

**Customer: Hey that is great, but we are just
looking around and not buying today.**

**Salesperson: No problem, most of my customers
don't purchase on the first visit. I will be happy
to show you around.**

There is no reason to try to close this customer on
buying today. They are pretty convinced that their
plan is not to buy today. Also they haven't been sold

on anything so what would they close on? Many salespeople lose right here because they don't want to waste their time and broom the customer. Don't get trapped into the "what's it gonna take for you to buy today" syndrome. Heck, if the customer knew at that point, the business wouldn't need salespeople. All you are really doing is pushing your customer to another dealership for someone else to make a sale and get a commission. In 23 years there has only been a few times that a customer walked in and said "I'm here to buy a car, who wants to sell one!" By the way, most of them had bad credit and couldn't buy anything anyway. Let the customer feel good about thinking they are in control and remember it is your mission to sell them today, don't buy the story so easily. You just need to have belief in your selling process and understand that this is just the first common objection to deal with.

SECOND STANDARD COMMON OBJECTION

At this point the customer may tell you that what they want to do is get their very best price on a vehicle and possibly know what they can get for their trade. If you run to the sales desk with a stock number and a trade appraisal at this time, you are going to fail. Remember logical thinking verses emotional thinking. You haven't sold the customer on you, your dealership, or a vehicle. Not only are you going to get a verbal whipping from the sales manager for not doing your job correctly, you will have to go back out to the customer and try to figure out how to explain that you couldn't get them the information and then continue with the sales process. Wave bye-bye to them, they are not coming back and neither is your commission.

So how do we handle the second standard common objection?

Customer: What we really want is the very best price on a vehicle and to find out what you will give us on trade for our car.

Salesperson: Hey, that is no problem at all! Remember I told you my job is to help you find a vehicle that will fill all your needs, wants, and desires and then get you that very best price. Not only the price, I will also be able to tell you how much we can pay you for your trade, how much money down you will need, if any at all, the monthly payment, term of the loan and your interest rate. We can get you all this information before you leave today, is that fair?

By disarming the objection by agreeing to it allows you, the salesperson, to take control of the selling process and get the customer into the inventory. Selling outside, closing inside. You have to tell the customer that for you to get them the best deal, the need to be on a vehicle that they would consider owning and allow you, the salesperson, to work with the managers to get them the best deal. Listen to understand the response from the customer. They may tell you that they are paying cash and interest rate, payment and terms doesn't matter. The customer may even approach the subject of rebates as down payments in lieu of cash down payment, which might indicate they have no money down. The customer may tell you that they have a pre approved draft check from their bank or credit union. You should be able to know from listening to the customers on how they plan to pay for the vehicle, whether the dealership will set up the financing or the customer is going to handle their financing or possibly paying cash. As your gathering all this information you must be able to retain it. As your experience grows, you will realize that controlling the sales process is based on the information and assumptions you extrapolate from your customer. Your goal is to get them looking at vehicles and off the numbers or pricing. You cannot close what is not sold and selling is your goal at this point. Your real intention is to share all the numbers with the customer when they are signing all the paperwork to take ownership.

The customer at this point should feel a bit more relaxed with you. They threw two objections and you handled them professionally and directly. You may get the third most common standard objection because the customer is hoping will scare you into giving the lowest price right up front.

THIRD COMMON STANDARD OBJECTION

Customer: I really appreciate everything, but you know we are going to still shop around after this.

Salesperson: That's ok, most smart buyers do. The process of shopping is to eliminate people who you won't do business with and vehicles you wouldn't consider, wouldn't you agree?

Now that you have called them smart for wanting to shop, you should be walking tall and feel in control of the sale. The customer, if they have shopped, probably feels pretty good about how this has gone so far. Just to mention, this all could happen in the first 3 minutes of greeting a customer. You only have one time for a first impression and you need to make it a good one. Prepare yourself by rehearsing the greeting and how to handle the common objections. Your confidence will go up every time you greet a customer and take them to the next step in the sales process.

Now what happens if you go to greet a customer and they put their hand up and say they don't want a salesperson? I suggest to smile at them and say that is ok, but you would like to give them you business card in case they have a question. Then you also mention they you will stay close enough to them so they won't have to search for you. If you stay within 30 feet, the customer will engage you into a conversation within a couple of minutes. Because you have disarmed the customer from his best defense, the customer will feel more comfortable with you and will feel you are not threat. Once you engage the customer, start the steps to a sale. Most salespeople will walk away from this customer stating they "don't want to waste their time." I have had many customers like this purchase from us by handling this way. Remember to smile, listen to understand, and stay in control.

2 COMMON GROUND AND INFORMATION

The timing of this step co-mingles with most of the selling steps. As you have already read, by handling the standard common objections you may have gathered important information that will help you to sell a car and make a commission. It is very important for you, the salesperson, to start getting on common ground with your customer as soon as you can. Customers will not buy from somebody they don't like. The goal of this step is to become familiar with your customers while gathering information that will help you select a vehicle and how to close them. If you try to interrogate your customer on the lot by blasting them with a bunch of questions, you are probably going to lose the sale. No one likes to be interrogated by a stranger.

Look at the vehicle the customer drove into the dealership. You should be looking for any member stickers or indicators. These could include Military, Golf Clubs, Housing Associations, Parking Permits, personalized license plates and the list can go on. Often you can start a casual conversation after the greeting by observing the stickers. People who are willing to put stickers on their car are always willing to talk about themselves. Here is the tricky part of common ground and information, you will need to listen to understand, do not listen just to respond. If you are just listening to respond, you are thinking of a response while the customer is talking to you which make it hard for you to listen and you will miss free information. Many times while having casual conversation the customer will inadvertently spill the secret to the deal without knowing it. For example, you have been talking to your customer about their job. You always need to be listening intently and compliment the subject. All of a sudden your customer states that he just got a raise and now can afford $500 per month for a new vehicle. That little tidbit of information will come in handy in the near future, and it also helps with selection of vehicle. Another possible scenario is that the customer states that the car they drove up in is a rental and their car was totaled in an accident. What you are trying to establish is if your customer is a need buyer or a want buyer. A need buyer is one that needs to purchase a car as soon as possible. This customer did not plan to buy a car and was injected into the market due to an unpredictable situation. This customer is very responsive to a professional, well informed and confident salesperson. A want buyer is very slow and never in a rush to buy a car. They enjoy doing all the research online and in dealerships. I have witnessed a couple that came into my dealership every weekend for 6 weeks just to drive a different vehicles. This customer may take 30 to 60 days to make a buying decision, but you must always assume that you can sell them a car today and make that your goal. There is no pay at a dealership for being a tour director.

A common mistake that is fatal to most sales is to ignore the spouse. If a couple is present, make sure your engaging both into the conversation.

During this step it is very wise to give the customer a tour of the service and parts area. Introduce them to a Service Writer and explain any awards or certifications that the service department holds. Make sure you know the history of the dealership and share that with the customers. The more comfortable they feel, the closer you are to selling a vehicle. You have to sell you, the vehicle and the dealership in order to make a sale.

Here is a list of common ground questions and what information you may retrieve.

1) What made you decide to come to ABC Motors today?

> They may have heard an ad on the radio, saw an ad in the newspaper or TV.
>
> A friend just purchased a car here.
>
> They have purchased here before.
>
> Have a car in the service department.
>
> Parents always purchased cars here.
>
> The customer was referred by a friend.
>
> Just drove by and saw a vehicle that they are interested in.

2) What kind of work do you do?

> Find out what type of work they do. You should be able to assume what type of income bracket they are in. If the customer works at a fast food restaurant, they probably make between $1400 and $1800 per month. If the customer is an attorney or doctor you can assume their income also. Now if both customers were looking at a brand new car that had an MSRP of $30,000.00, who do you think will qualify easier?

Find out employment information on all buyers present. Remember, don't ignore the spouse.

3) Will you be replacing a vehicle or just adding another one?

Will let you know if they are trading.

Will let you know if the trade is here.

If not trading, but replacing, prior vehicle in an accident.

Will tell you who the car is for. Not trading, but buying a car for a teenager.

Sometimes will tell you why they are trading.

May mention service problems with car.

Want or need buyer.

4) Who will be the primary driver of your new vehicle?

Will let you know who to sell to.

Will let you know who the buyer is and who the decision maker is.

5) How soon do you plan on making a buying decision?

This actually puts the customer at ease because it makes them feel like you're not pressuring them.

Sometimes the customer will have a time limit due to source of funds coming in.

The customer may be in the middle of getting a mortgage for a new home.

6) What side of town do you live on?

Could let you figure out how many dealerships they could have shopped at on the way to your dealership.

Customers that have driven a long way are more committed buyers.

During the first two steps of the sale, and sometimes a little farther down the sales process, you may be tempted to ask the customer "how is your credit?" That will be a big mistake on your part. Many customers with good credit will be offended, feeling that you just want to know if they can buy or feel it is an invasion of their privacy. For people with bad or slow credit, you may put them in a position where they won't tell you the truth, which at one point during the closing steps they will realize you will find out that they lied to you and won't close because of that. Either way you have set up the customer for the next salesperson at another dealership to earn your commission. Sometimes people who think they have marginal credit are incorrect and you do not want to run off a customer that can buy a car. A customer with derogatory credit will usually bring it up to you before you ever go on a demonstration drive. They may ask about special credit programs, in house or secondary financing. Remember listen to understand, not to just respond? In the dealerships that I worked in, we developed a pre-approval form for customers that were concerned by their credit. Whenever a customer brought up concerns about credit, we would offer them an opportunity to pre-qualify in 5 minutes with no cost to them. The form was designed for us to know income, time on job, time on residence, down payment, trade in, trade payoff, and desired payment. It also allowed us to run a credit bureau on the customer. The managers then could tell the salesperson what or what we couldn't do with the customer. Check with your managers to find out the policy in your dealership on how they handle credit customers. This is extremely important; always assume that a customer can buy until proven else wise. There are many stories that float around every dealership on how somebody came to the dealership looking like they didn't have two nickels to rub together and they turned out to have enough money to buy the dealership and ended up buying a vehicle at full price. Luck has nothing to do with it. If you want a commission, follow the sales process. Short cuts equal short paychecks. You choose how much you want to make every day.

One of the most embarrassing times for a salesperson is when they have been with a customer for a while and can't remember the customer's name. When you ask their name again or use the wrong name, just watch the smile leave their face. If you have problems with names, like most of us do, get yourself a pocket note pad and when you have finished your introductions, tell the customers that you would like to take a second and write their names down. Sometimes you can even ask for a contact phone number at this point. I believe that most customers will appreciate the professionalism that you are demonstrating at this point by showing how important they are to you. Unfortunately you will run into the customer that won't give you their name much less a phone number. All you can do is smile real big, and ask the customer how you should refer to them. Be polite and continue on the sale process. Either the ice will break or there wasn't anything you could do with this customer. If you have a name and a contact number, you have a prospect for follow-up if you don't sell them now. If you don't have a name and a number, you don't have a prospect. Many dealerships require salespeople to wear name tags. If your dealership doesn't require you to wear one, I would suggest going to a nearby mall or trophy shop and have one made. The best one is the tag that holds on by magnets, not pins. The reason for a name tag is the way most dealerships operate. If you have a customer that comes into the dealership and doesn't ask for you and buys a vehicle, you don't receive any credit or commissions. This usually happens on your day off. The customer you spent 3 hours with a couple of days ago decides that the car you showed them is the one they want. However he cannot recall your name and he has tossed your card so he just pops in assuming that you would be there. As he is greeted by a co-worker he mentions that he spoke with someone the other day but can't remember the name. The new salesperson runs really fast through the names in the sales staff and the customer states he is unsure. Free customer! All your hard work went to making another salespersons job that much easier. Normally if the customer does ask for you and your not there you still receive half credit for the sale and half the commission. The real bad part is if you miss an end of the month bonus by half a unit. What is the lesson here? Get a name tag and wear it.

I recommend getting business cards a.s.a.p. even if you have to pay for them. Because of high turnover of new salespeople in the first sixty days, most dealerships won't order business cards for that period of time. The more people you hand business cards to the better your odds are at selling a vehicle. Don't be shy about being a salesperson, let everyone know and give them your business card. Most salespeople only staple their business card to a brochure to a departing customer. This is called the getaway package. The brochure will end up on a table in the house or the backseat of the car, and so will your business card. I have found that you can have pens made with a logo, name and number for not much more than business cards. Also recently, I found out that almost nobody will discard a set of nail clippers. They can also be done with a logo, name and number. In this business, it is ok to be different.

3 SELECT A VEHICLE

Selection of a vehicle can be as easy as the customer holding an ad in their hand asking to see a particular vehicle, or as hard as the customer saying "don't really know what I want." Both situations have their own perils.

For instance, a customer comes in and requests to see a particular vehicle that was advertised in the newspaper. You introduce yourself and proceed with the customer out to the vehicle. The customer looks at the vehicle and states that it has too many miles and thanks you for your time and asks for a business card. Now here come the choices. Give the customer a card, get their name and number in case you get another vehicle in with lower miles. You could do this, but chances of selling this customer will be very slim unless you get a vehicle in that day or the next. This customer is searching in the newspaper for a vehicle and probably has other vehicles to look at. Here is the better way of handling this situation.

Customer: Oh this vehicle has too many miles, I appreciate your time, and can I get a business card?

Salesperson: Sure, no problem, but can I ask you a question?

Customer: Yes.

Salesperson: What interested you the most about this vehicle, the price or the make and model?

Customer: Well I was looking for a vehicle in that price range.

Salesperson: Ok, were you planning on paying cash?

Customer: Yea, I only have that much money to work with and didn't want to finance.

Salesperson: Great, before you leave I would like to show you a couple of other vehicles that have lower mileage that we should be able to get you a great deal.

Customer: OK!

In this example you probably have realized that you need to know your inventory very well. I would encourage you to find out what vehicles have come in each day. New vehicles and used vehicles purchased at an auction will come in on trucks called car carriers. Watch for those all the time. Trade-ins appear all the time. Most dealerships have a process for handling all incoming vehicles and are generally staged in one area prior to Pre Delivery Inspection, reconditioning and detail. Taking a stroll through this area a couple of times a day will keep you up on your inventory and you might find a vehicle for a recent prospect. Sell a car, make a commission!

With this customer we need to show a different vehicle to. You should keep in mind the dollar amount they want to spend and keep your selection within that price range. As soon as you show them a vehicle they will immediately ask "how much is this vehicle?" Sometimes you will be showing a vehicle that has a price on it higher than what they wanted. You need to tell the customer that they shouldn't worry about price, because you are going to tell the manager that they came in on the newspaper ad, but didn't like the vehicle. Usually the manager will work a great price in that case on another vehicle. Usually if the customer is sold well enough on the switch vehicle and on you then they will pay more than they said they would. If price was the only determining factor in a buying decision the mileage would not have been a factor on the first vehicle. Listen to understand not to respond.

This process will also work if the customer inquires about a car that has been sold. You could say, "Sorry that has been sold" and watch the customer leave, or you can say to the customer "Ok, come on inside and let me check the availability of that vehicle." Once inside you start on this process again.

What about the customer who states they have no idea what they want. I have watched salespeople flip a business card at the customer and tell them if they find something on the lot there interested in to come get them. That is a sure way of not making a commission. I never thought selling by ignoring worked. The better way of handling this customer is by being patient and make sure you are on the top of your game with product knowledge and enthusiasm. Let's see how to handle this customer in an example conversation.

Customer: I really don't have a clue what I am looking for. There are so many makes and models.

Salesperson: I understand. There are many makes and models out in the market today. How familiar are you with the models we carry?

Customer: Not much, I have seen some commercials on them.

Salesperson: Really, which commercial did you see?

Customer: The one on the ____model.

Salesperson: That is a great model. I have one over here if you would like to look at it.

Customer: That would be great!

Still remember, this may not be the vehicle that the customer is interested in. If the customer follows you in the next steps of the sale, assume that you may be on the right vehicle.

If the customer will not do what you want them to do, then you have a problem. The problem could be you, the vehicle, or the pricing. They are the three most prevalent reasons why a customer does not buy a vehicle from you. If you show a vehicle to a customer and they refuse to go on a demonstration drive, it is possible that you're on the wrong vehicle. You might as well just put it out there now. Ask your customer if the vehicle is ok. Let's see how this conversation would go.

Salesperson: Great, let me go ahead and get the vehicle ready for a demonstration drive.

Customer: No thanks, we don't want to drive it. We would just like your best price.

At this point, I believe that the customer just wants to leave. No matter what price you give them, they will say "ok, can you write that down on your business card." The reality is they don't like the vehicle so don't buy the "we don't need to drive it" story. Many of these customers actually don't know how to tell you that they don't like the vehicle and it is up to you to find out.

Salesperson: hey folks, you won't hurt my feelings if you don't like this vehicle. I sort of sense that may be a problem. Is it?

Customer: Well, actually we really don't like the color.

Salesperson: Other than the color, is there anything else you don't like about it?

Customer: No, it is a nice looking vehicle, but this color is terrible.

Salesperson: OK, other than this color, what is another color that you wouldn't have?

Most models come in six to eight colors. By asking what color they wouldn't have gives you more choices than asking what color they want. If you ask what color they want, and you don't have it your sale is starting to spin apart.

Customer: Green.

Salesperson: Great, let's walk out here into the inventory and see what other colors we have.

Customer: OK!

Now your back on the sales process and your chances of selling a vehicle just went up. This will also work on model dislikes, different options or pricing. Just restate the objection to the customer as a closing question. For example,

Customer: I really don't want a sunroof.

Salesperson: So if I understand you correctly, if we have a vehicle like this without a sunroof you would consider owning it?

Customer: I would consider it more than one with a sunroof.

Salesperson: Super, I have other vehicles in stock without a sunroof, let's go and look at them.

Once you have a customer in the inventory, they will normally start telling you what they want and don't want. It is up to you to know your inventory well enough to direct the customer to the correct vehicle.

What happens on a new vehicle when you don't have what the customer wants? The customer has picked out a vehicle, but it is the wrong color and will not choose a different color. If you have exhausted all attempts at a different color then the only way to save your deal is by offering a dealer trade. A dealer trade is where two dealerships swap vehicles. This is a function of management. The way to set your deal up so it will go smoothly on a dealer trade is quite simple. You should tell your customers that the dealership can swap inventory with another dealership to get exactly what they want with no extra cost to them. The process for this is to find a vehicle on the lot that is equipped as close as to the way the customer desires and then when you do the write it up, you acknowledge that the dealership will need to dealer trade this unit for one with the color that the customer desires. On the write up form use the word "LIKE" before the stock number and when

BRUCE BELLIS

you take the write up to the sales desk, make sure the manager knows that it is a dealer trade deal and that you are providing the stock number of the vehicle on your lot that was closest to what the customer wanted. In many cases the customer will get so excited about buying a vehicle that they will go ahead and take the one you have in stock so they don't have to wait. Sell what you see; don't see what you can sell!

What about the customer that comes in and requests to look at a particular model, but is unfamiliar with trim levels and engine options. This customer has looked at a model on the road, or on a television commercial but hasn't really studied the car. You should take the customer out into the inventory and explain the different model trim levels in that line. Start by showing the base model vehicle first and as you start your static presentation the customer may start inquiring about more equipment. Once you verify that the customer is looking for more equipment or higher trim level then go up to the next trim level or even the top level if the customer seems to be interested in it. In this case it may take a demonstration drive in each vehicle for the customer to make a decision.

Some customers will come in and tell you that they are looking for a vehicle with a $300.00 payment with $500.00 down. No dealership keeps a list of inventory for this query. There are too many variables that figure into a retail installment contract to be able to know what lender the customer will qualify for. What you should do with this customer is to take them into the used vehicle inventory, find a vehicle that is 2 to 3 years old and sells for less than $10000.00. Tell the customer that these vehicles should get them around there target and then start the sales process. If the customer doesn't like the vehicles then start showing them vehicles that are slightly more. If the customer asks you what the payments will be on this vehicle just tell them they will be just a little bit higher. If they continue the customer has "bumped" their target payment. Remember, if the payment was the only decision factor, they would take any vehicle that would fit that payment. Since they didn't like the first vehicle, you can assume as long as the payment is within reason the customer will pay more for the vehicle that they are sold on and desire.

Whatever the situation is with the customer, always remember that you have to settle them down on a particular vehicle if you will have any chance of selling them a vehicle. When the customer will not do what you want them to do, you have a problem. That problem could be one of three reasons. The customers do not like you. The customers do not like the vehicle. The customers do not like the pricing. You need to be able to recognize body language and realize when a customer is not interested in the vehicle your showing. During the next step of the sale you will see how important it is to get the customer involved in the vehicle. Remember logical thinking verses emotional thinking. The next step is where you really work on the emotional side of the customer.

4 STATIC PRESENTATION

Static is defined as not moving, presentation is defined as showing an item or items. Vehicles do not sell themselves. I know this to be true because dealerships need salespeople. Unfortunately many salespeople open a car door, let the customer sit inside while they hang on the door and ask the customer "what ya think?"

A static presentation is the step that you should use all your enthusiasm and product knowledge. Humans have five senses. Sight, smell, taste, touch and hearing. In order to get the customers logical thinking down and the emotional thinking up, we need to use most of the human senses.

Feature-Benefit Presentation. The best way to do a presentation on a vehicle is by explaining every feature and what the benefit is to the customer. This is also called value selling.

Whether you are verbalizing a feature or physically demonstrating a feature you always explain the benefit to the customer as this builds value. Also if the customer has been to another dealership they will be impressed by your product knowledge and that only puts you closer to a sale.

When starting a static presentation on a vehicle you will need to isolate that vehicle from the other inventory. If the dealership is not equipped with a presentation area, then you need to find a place on the lot to show the vehicle away from the other vehicles. It is important that while you are doing your presentation, the customer starts looking at the car in the next row.

Prepare your presentation by opening all the doors, the hood and the trunk. The vehicle should be off and the keys in your pocket. Many salespeople have had customers accidentally close the doors at the end of the presentation and have locked the keys in the car.

Start your presentation at the Window Sticker. On new vehicles the Maroney Sticker not only shows the price of the vehicle, it describes all optional and standard equipment, safety items, fuel cost and miles per gallon estimates. Remember to explain the feature or option and the benefit to the customer. The Window Sticker will tell the customer about the warranty on the vehicle as well as roadside assistance. Spend time on the window sticker and have the customers look at it with you. Point out the information on the sticker and ask them if they have any questions.

Next step is under the hood. Explain engine features, horse power, torque, where to check fluids, oil etc. Again, get the customer involved. On the right side of the car you can have the customers touch the paint and explain the paint process the factory uses and the body rust perforation warranty that comes with the vehicle. In the trunk area, show where spare tire and tools are, cubic feet of space and how it compares to other cars in the same class. Some vehicles have folding back seats as a feature to increase trunk space. If the vehicle is so equipped, then demonstrate it to the customer and explain the benefit. Once you move the primary driver into the driver's seat, go over all interior options and features and explain the benefits of those features and options. Ask the customer how it feels, how does the seat feel, does the steering wheel feel comfortable? The more you have the customer touch and feel the car the more emotional they are getting about it.

Used cars, certified cars, pre-owned vehicles sell basically the same way. Most dealers have a service to put the Federal Trade Commission Buyers Guide in the window and usually will explain the warranty on the vehicle and the optional equipment. An important factor to remember and to share with a customer is what they are paying for on a used vehicle. It is the remainder of the serviceable life of the vehicle. So it would make sense that vehicles that are very old and ones with very high miles are cheaper because the serviceable life remaining is much shorter. A vehicle that has lower miles or has a certification warranty has a longer remaining serviceable life and that is why they are more expensive. It is also important to know the reconditioning process and policy of the dealership. It never hurts to share with a customer what services and inspections are done on used vehicles prior to placing them on the lot for sale. If your dealership subscribes to a vehicle history service, make sure you let your customer know that they can get that information.

A good static presentation should last 15 to 25 minutes or so. Any longer and you may become boring. Have flexibility in your presentation to present what is important to your customer. If you're showing a high performance vehicle to a customer, they may not be too interested in the size of the trunk. If you are showing a Soccer Mom a

van, she may want to know more about safety and
security items than the bore and stroke of the
engine. Always analyze your customer and tailor
your presentation to your customer's needs, wants
and desires. Remember to watch the customer's
body language or the loss of attention to the vehicle
as it may be an indication the customer might not
like the vehicle. If the customer won't do what you
want them to do, you have a problem. The problem
could be you, the vehicle or the price. As you
transition to the demonstration ride you should very
alert for apprehension with the customer. If you run
into a problem at this point, you may have to start
over with information and select a different vehicle.

5 DEMONSTRATION RIDE

Before you go on a demonstration ride you need to be prepared. Often dealerships will have a pre-determined demo route. The route is usually designed for lack of traffic, smoothness of the road surface, distance and an area where you can switch drivers. You should become familiar with the demo route by driving the route many times. If the dealership does not have an established demonstration route you will need to come up with one. You should have the route designed to go on smooth roads with as little traffic as possible. At the half way point you should have a parking lot or a park to do your turnaround. Sometimes by asking the senior salespeople what route they use could be very useful to you. Make sure you are familiar with the route. You don't want to get lost while on a demonstration ride.

Most dealerships require the salesperson to make a photocopy of the customer's driver's license before the demonstration drive. I directed my salespeople to write down their name, the stock number of the vehicle that they are demonstrating, and the current time on the photocopy of the customer's driver's license and leave it with the sales manager. Dealer License Plates are usually issued at the sales desk and you should retrieve one for your demonstration drive. Make sure that there is enough fuel in the vehicle. One sure fire way to kill a deal is to run out of gas while on the demonstration ride. Find out from your managers on how to get fuel for a vehicle. Dealerships rarely have their own fuel tanks on the dealership property and will often have a relationship with a local service station. If the vehicle is in need of fuel, alter your demonstration drive and take your customers with you. It is not a good idea to leave them standing around the dealership while you go get fuel. More often than not when you get back they have left. Customer control is a key factor for a successful sale.

After you have prepared for a demonstration ride, you should follow certain rules. The first rule is that the customer never goes on a demonstration ride by themselves. There are a couple of reasons for this. One reason is that you will not have any control where they drive or how long it will take. It also will give the customer the time to start thinking logically again. They will start to remind each other that they didn't come to buy, only to look and get a price. If you are in the vehicle, that type of conversation will hardly ever come up. The worst situation is when you have to explain to a sales manager that the customers you put out on a demonstration have been gone for six hours and you can't get a hold of them. Once the police leave after doing the stolen car report, you will probably be asked to leave also.

The second rule is that the customer never drives off the lot. The customer is unfamiliar with vehicle operation as well as the roads and streets. You want the customer to enjoy the vehicle and not to be distracted by looking for traffic or following instructions on where to drive. By starting the demonstration drive with you driving will also give you more control over the customer.

The third rule is to never take a vehicle off of the paved roads. There are many four wheel drive vehicles and sport utilities in the market today and customers may ask to take the vehicle off road. Unless your dealership doesn't have a policy against taking off road demonstration drive you should tell the customer that is against company policy. The vehicle can get damaged on off road drives as well as getting stuck. In either case, your deal will die with your career will be left out in the field.

The fourth rule is to never break the speed limit and to follow all traffic signs and instructions. This rule applies to you and your customers. I think it is very appropriate to inform your customers who are driving unlawfully that you insist that drive the vehicle lawfully. You have to smile when you're telling them or they may get upset at you. Be realistic, doing 60 in a 55 is not what I am referring to, however doing 70 in a 45 requires a conversation.

The fifth rule is to inform your customers on how the demonstration ride will proceed. It should go something like this.

Salesperson: Ok folks; let's get ready to go for a demonstration drive. By policy I will need to make a copy of your driver's licenses and I will need to get a Dealer Plate. When we go on the demonstration drive I will drive the vehicle to an area off the lot where we can switch drivers, is that ok?

Customer: Can we drive it buy ourselves?

Salesperson: I'm sorry, that is against our policy.

Customer: Ok, but will we both get to drive it?

Salesperson: Absolutely!

Remember to smile when you are speaking with your customers, it will put them at ease.

Direct the primary driver of the vehicle to the front passenger seat and anyone else to the rear seats. You get into the driver's seat and instruct everyone to buckle their seatbelts.

As you start the demonstration ride, the radio should be turned off. Last thing you want your customers to hear is a competitor's advertisement at this point. Tell the customer the route you are driving and how long it will be before you stop to switch drivers. You should be talking and keeping the customers attention on the vehicle and its features. Also mention the ride and feel of the vehicle. Again this is a selling step and you are trying to get the customer in an emotional state of mind. Interact with your customers and ask them questions as to ride and feel. You want them to be involved as much as possible. Have them adjust the Air Conditioning or Heater controls. Have the customer open the glove compartment and console to visually inspect the storage size. Ask them how the seat feels and do they feel comfortable.

If the customer turns the radio on don't make them turn it off. When you get to the turnaround area you can turn the radio off then.

Once you get to the turnaround area, try to find a shady spot to park under. Turn off the motor and remove the keys from the ignition. Keep the keys in your hand. You don't want to get locked out now. Get the customer to stand back from the vehicle and take a look at it. Make sure you make positive comments about the vehicle and ask the customer if they agree.

Have the primary driver get into the driver's seat and assist them in making sure that the seat is adjusted correctly and that they have their seatbelt on. If you have another person, they should sit in the front passenger seat and you should get into the back seat. Make sure everyone is buckled up and then give the keys to the driver. Ask the driver to make sure that all the mirrors are adjusted correctly and then instruct the customer to where to drive.

Your selling part is coming to an end. On the return drive to the dealership you should only answer questions from the customer or to instruct them on where to drive. What you are hoping for is that the customer will start to take mental ownership of the vehicle. The more silent you are the better it is. Upon return to the dealership be prepared to tell the customer where to park. I do not suggest that you have them park the vehicle back into the inventory area. Have them park in front of the dealership. If the dealership has a sold vehicle parking area, just have the customer park there by directing them to it and not by verbally referring to it as a sold vehicle area.

Now that we are back at the dealership you are about to go to the next step in the sale, the Trial Close. But before we do that, we need to recap what we have done up to this point. You have completed the first five steps of the steps to a sale. With the proper amount of product knowledge, inventory information and a selling attitude you have found a prospect to talk with. You approached them with a brisk walk and a smile on your face. You remember the prompt and friendly greeting. You welcomed them to the dealership and ask if they came for the big sale. After proper introductions and asking permission to write their names down you explain what your job is at the dealership and what you will do for them. The customer gives you one or all of the three standard common objections and you handle them accordingly. You know the next step is common ground and information and as you begin a conversation with the customer, they tell you they are interested in a used car and give you the dollar amount they want to spend. While you and the customer select a vehicle you realize the importance of knowing your inventory as the customer has requested a vehicle in a certain price range. You also find out if they will have a trade in or not and whether they plan to finance the vehicle or pay cash. Once a vehicle has been selected, you isolate the vehicle from the other inventory and do a static presentation. You tell the customer that you are planning on taking them on a demonstration drive and company policy requires a copy of their driver's licenses. When you leave your customer to make copies of their licenses you realize that the less time you spend away from the customer is better. You make a note on the photocopy of the driver's license with your name, the stock number of the vehicle and the current time. You acquire a Dealer License plate and quickly return to the customer. You tell the customer the route you will take and that you will drive the vehicle off the lot to an area where you can switch drivers. Remember the five rules of the demonstration drive and proceed. You complete the switching of drivers and return to the dealership. What you hope to have succeeded in is to have a customer that is sold on you, the vehicle, and the dealership and to have their emotional thinking so high that they will buy the vehicle now.

If at any point the customer will not do what you want them to do, i.e. go to the next step in the sale, then you have a problem. The problem is the vehicle, the pricing or you. Don't be so quick to "buy the story." The word "be-back" came from customers making excuses to leave the lot and telling the salesperson that they will "be-back." The truth is that most of these customers never come back because they didn't like the car or the pricing or you.

Try to go back to common ground and information and find out where your deal is going sour.

If the customer persists and wants to leave the dealership at any step in the sale you need help. Getting someone else to speak with your customers is called a "TO." "TO" is a turnover. You are turning your customer over to another salesperson, sales manager, closer or a finance manager. Most dealerships have two types of "TO" procedures. One is done by other salespeople, which if they get the deal back on track and get it closed they will get half your deal. The other procedure is that a sales manager or another manager or closer goes in and tries to get your deal back on track. If they succeed it generally doesn't cost you half a deal. Some dealerships have mandatory "TO" policy and if you don't adhere to it you are jeopardizing your job. Other dealerships have a "TO" policy, but only enforce it when upper management is around and some dealerships don't have a policy at all. Make sure you understand the dealerships policy where you work and follow it. I would suggest that you start in a dealership with a mandatory "TO" policy. I have watched the egos of salespeople lose them a ton of money in commissions because they didn't want to "TO" their customer. These are the salespeople who buy the story that the customer will be-back. The only thing a "TO" can do for you is to put money into your pocket. Face it, the customer was leaving and you don't get paid to be a tour director. Another possibly is that a more experienced salesperson will sniff out the real objection and put the deal back together. Now you made a commission. As the old saying goes "a half of a loaf is better than none at all." Don't let your ego cost you money, "TO" every customer whatever the dealership policy is.

6 TRIAL CLOSE

What is a trial close? It is a set of questions and assumptions from you to the customer to verify that the customer does not have any viable objections to the vehicle that has been selected. It also verifies that the customer is receptive to the idea of buying the vehicle from you.

You can just come out with "Do ya think you wanna buy it?" You will surely get a no to a very direct question. You will be much more successful by asking indirect questions that will lead to an assumption that the customer is ready to buy. Your customer is already a bit nervous at this point due to the fact that they know that after the demonstration ride someone is going to ask them to buy a car. So by asking indirect questions will not get you a negative answer. You should make sure that the customers are outside of the car and that you are close to them. You need to make sure that you control the situation at this point. Some salespeople lose their deal here because they never ask for the trial close and the customer leaves the dealership stating that they want to think about it. The trail close should go like this.

Salesperson: Well folks, how did you like how it drove?

Customer: Oh it drove real well.

Salesperson: And the color is the color ok?

Customer: The color is great!

Salesperson: Is the vehicle equipped the way you want?

Customer: Sure is.

Salesperson: Well then, let's go inside and let me show you how easy it is to purchase a vehicle from ABC Motors!

Start heading for the door to the showroom and hold it open for your customers. If they follow you then they have trial closed. If they don't follow you, try to "nudge" them buy looking and them and asking them to come in the showroom again. If that doesn't work, then you have a problem and the problem is you, or the car, or the pricing. Time to start asking questions to save your deal.

Sometimes the customer just doesn't want to commit but are interested. This is a great time to tell the customer that you want to stay by your word and give them all the information on their best price, how much we can pay for their trade and details of financing and that you understand that they don't want to make a purchasing decision right now. This allows you to remain in control and bring the customers inside. This assumptive trial close only works if the customer is sold on you and the vehicle. Nobody buys from somebody they don't like and a vehicle they dislike. Once inside the showroom, walk the customer over to your work area and have them have a seat. Make sure they are comfortable and offer a beverage to them.

If you have tried both indirect and assumptive trail closes and the customer wants to leave you should get a TO. Often you can ask the customer to wait a moment so you can get them a brochure. This will allow you the time to go to the sales desk and ask for help. At this point you just follow the manager's direction.

7 TRADE APPRASIAL

If the customer has a trade you can assume that they have done some research on the value of their vehicle. You can also assume that they searched for the highest value they could find. Whether they have looked on the internet, car value books, or newspaper ads, rest assured that the customer did not take in account the condition of their vehicle when establishing a value. This is why it is important to your deal that you complete a trade appraisal with the customer. At the end of the trade appraisal with the customer you will take the vehicle to the Used Car buyer or designated appraiser to get a value so your deal can be worked. The dealership will have forms for trade appraisals and you need to fill it out with the customer.

Ask the customer for the keys to their trade. This insures you stay in control. Ask the customer to take you to their trade in. What you are about to do is called a silent appraisal and it makes the customer question if the value that they think the vehicle is worth is totally accurate. Your goal is to make sure that the customer is aware that you noticed the items that could devaluate the vehicle without verbally making mention of them. You need to tell the customer that you are gathering information to share with the Used Car Buyer so you can get top dollar. Once you are at the vehicle start completing the appraisal form. The form will usually have blanks for year, make, model, vehicle identification number, color, optional equipment

While you walk around the vehicle make sure you run your hand over any paint scratches, dents, dings, or imperfections. You should touch any cracks or star chips on the windshield or on any other windows. Physically check the tread depth on all the tires. Open the hood and visually inspect the engine compartment. Pull the oil dipstick and look at the color of the oil. Ask the customer if you can open the trunk to check the spare tire. Sit inside the vehicle and do a visual inspection. Touch any stains, tears, burn holes or any other imperfections on the interior. Once you have completed the walk around with the customer you should ask a few questions. You should ask the customer if the vehicle has had any damage history and if it had what the repair cost was. Also ask if their vehicle has any type of mechanical warranty that could transfer to a new owner.

Use some common sense when doing the silent appraisal. If the vehicle is 10 years old with 250000 miles on it, you probably don't have to worry about doing an extensive silent appraisal. The silent appraisal works well on vehicles that will end up for sale on your pre-owned lot after they are traded.

You should take your customer back to your work area at this time and make sure they are comfortable. Let them know that you are going to take their vehicle to the Used Car Buyer for appraisal. Some dealerships require that the salesperson stay with the appraiser throughout the appraisal process while others don't. My recommendation is that if the dealership you work for doesn't require you to accompany the appraiser then you should go back to your customers and start preparing your write up form. In my experience this is a time when salespeople want to stand outside and talk with other salespeople about their deal. The other salespeople will start asking questions about the customer and what they are trading and what they owe on it, what kind of credit and the list goes on. While this chattering is absolutely useless, your customer is watching you and the others. If they interpret your actions or mannerisms as insincere it will hurt your ability to close this deal. Remember that the customer is always watching you and you don't want to do anything that can hurt you chance for a sale. A good rule is never to leave your customer alone when you don't have to.

8 WRITE UP

This is the step where you reduce the entire transaction to paper. The write up form is a closing tool as well as a negotiating tool. This form is how you present the deal to the Sales Manager and to the customer. As stated earlier, the selling part is over and the closing part has started.

Every time that the customer agrees with you or gives you information you are closer to closing the deal. The write up form will usually require the following information.

Buyer name

Co-Buyer Name

Address, City, State, Zip

Buyer Date of Birth

Co-Buyer date of Birth

Home, work and cell phone numbers

Drivers License numbers

Insurance policy information

Information on the vehicle that you are selling

Information on the trade in vehicle

Payoff amount on trade in with payoff information

You will find that having a note pad that you carry in your pocket will save you walking and diminish the time you are away from the customer. When you are on the demonstration ride you should be writing down the stock number to the vehicle you are in. Also write down the year, make, model, vehicle identification number, color and actual mileage. You should have the same information on the trade in from when you did your appraisal.

How you complete the write up form is more important they the content of the form. Some salespeople will just ask for the customer's driver's license and start filling out the form. The customers get to sit there and look at the top of their salespersons head in total silence for a number of minutes that feel like hours to them. As I mentioned, the write up is a closing tool and every time the customer gives you information you closer to a sale. Instead of filling out the form quietly get your customer involved. Here is an example of the exchange of information while completing the write up form.

Salesperson: Ok folks, the next step we need to do are to fill out an offer to purchase form. This will only take a few minutes and then I will get with the Sales Manager and get you that great deal I promised. Is that ok?

Customer: Sure, what do we need to do?

Salesperson: Well let's see, how would you like your new vehicle titled?

Customer: In my name and my wife's name.

Salesperson: OK, can I get your driver's licenses so I have the correct spelling? By the way, the

address on your license, is that the correct address to title your vehicle to?

Customer: Yes it is.

There were three closing questions in that exchange with the customer. The customer gave a positive response to all three. The first one was when the salesperson explained to the customer that he would get the great deal as promised and asked it was ok. The customer response was positive. The second was when asked how the customer would want there new vehicle titled. By giving the answer that the customer did, that is a positive. The last is confirming the titling address. You can fill out the rest of the form while asking questions. When it comes to the vehicle information, you need to develop the ability to write and talk at the same time. You also need to look up and make eye contact with your customers frequently during this step. Don't get caught up with filling out the form and ignoring the customer.

Dealerships will vary on what pricing numbers they want on the write up form so make sure you are aware of your dealership policies and follow them. I recommend that the List price of the vehicle you are selling is on the write up and the payoff amount of the trade if there is a payoff. You should never write down or ask about down payments or desired monthly payments. The reason for this is it is better to let the Sales Manager price the deal to the customer, not the other way around.

Now that the form is completed you have to take it to the Sales Manager to get the first "pencil." When you leave your work area tell the customer that you are going to the Sales Manager to get the figures and it will only be a couple of minutes.

When you go to the sales desk, make sure you have the write up form complete. Sales Managers are usually busy and are not into long boring conversations about your deal. You should tell them what you know about your customers. Facts such as where they plan on financing, desired payments, whether they have shopped other dealerships, and whether you have a hard commitment to purchase, or not is what the Sales Manager will listen to. All the other information will be ignored. Most of this information you will have gathered as you proceeded with the steps of the sale. Remember to listen to understand, not to respond?

The Sales Manager will then "pencil" the deal with the selling price, trade amount, cash down and monthly payments and will hand it back to you. The Sales Manager may explain the pricing and suggest a way to present it to the customer. The Sales Manager may also give you some information to share with the customer. This is called "loading your lips." The reason a person earns the title of Sales Manager is because they are very good at reading a deal and know how to direct the close. This means that if they "load your lips" be sure that you remember it correctly and share it with your customer as instructed.

9 PRESENT THE ORDER

Ok, now is the time the rubber meets the road. You have your write-up and the Sales Manager has "penciled" your deal. Now you must present it to your customers in a clear, concise and matter of fact manner. The key to a proper presentation is your state of mind. You have listened to your customer tell you that they want $5000 for their trade or that they have no money down, but the Sales Manager penciled the deal with $3000 for the trade and $2000 cash down. Your first thought is the customers are going to "blow out" as soon as they see that. Not true. If you have some self confidence and remember that you are the negotiator, not the decision maker, you will be able to control the close and sell a vehicle. On the next page is an example of a typical write-up.

POWER CAR SELLING FOR THE INEXPERIENCED SALESPERSON

Customer Name _____ Stock# _____ Salesperson_____

Address _____ (H) _____ (W) _____

City, St, Zip _____ (C) _____

VEHICLE TO BE PURCHASED

NEW/USED_____ YEAR _____ MAKE _____ MODEL _____ COLOR _____

VIN _____ MILEAGE _____

VEHICLE TO BE TRADED

YEAR _____ MAKE _____ MODEL _____ COLOR _____

VIN _____ MILEAGE _____

PAYOFF AMOUNT _____ PAYOFF LENDER _____

SALE PRICE	**TRADE ALLOWANCE**

CASH DOWN	**MONTHLY PAYMENTS**

THIS IS AN OFFER TO PURCHASE THE ABOVE DESCRIBED VEHICLE. THIS IS NOT A SALES CONTRACT. I (WE) AGREE TO PURCHASE THIS VEHICLE BASED ON THE ABOVE TERMS. SIGN HERE

X_____

The previous page has a form called an "Offer to Purchase" or "Deal Worksheet." The form is also called a 4-square by car people. As you can see it holds information on the customer and the vehicles involved. This is a very important form so you must make sure you fill it out accurately. I have had salespeople use a stock number of one car and thought they were selling another and at the end of the deal the customer blows up because they didn't get the car they wanted. Bye-Bye customer and commission.

Generally the only number you put into any of the 4-squares would be the list price of the vehicle you're selling. The sales manager will complete the other three squares and "load your lips" for the presentation of the order.

Presenting the order is simple if you practice. Presenting the order should follow a pattern. Present the price of the vehicle your selling, the trade allowance, cash down and the monthly payment in that order. When presenting the order always do it with both you and your customers sitting. An old superstition in the car business is that nobody will close if they are standing. Here is the word track for presenting the order.

Hey folks, come on over and have a seat. I just got the figures from my manager and I think you will be very happy!

Now using your pen as a pointer....

This is the sale price of ours, this is your trade allowance, cash down needed, and your monthly payments and all I need is your OK right here to get your new vehicle ready for delivery.

No verbalization of numbers. It is too much for the customer to here and sees and may confuse them. Keep it simple and to the point.

Once you have presented the order and asked for the signature commitment you must stay quiet. If you pay very close attention the customer will either sign it and you have a deal or they will tell you how to close them. The next step is to close the deal and we do that by negotiation.

10 THE CLOSE

Closing the deal can be easy or difficult depending on how well the customer is sold on you, the vehicle and the dealership. If you have done all the selling steps correctly the customer should close fast. If the customer won't close, then you need to get some help because there is a problem with your deal.

The secret to the close is an anagram "I I N O" That stands for Identify, Isolate, Negotiate and Overcome. What the customer states as a reply to the order is usually an objection. An objection is what we need to close. There may be more than one objection so that is the reason to Identify all objections and the Isolate them from the other numbers. Once that is accomplished we can Negotiate and Overcome the objection and have a commitment to purchase from the customer.

Here is an example close.

Customer: "Is that all you can give me for my trade?"

Salesperson: "I'm not sure, but are there any other concerns on this paper?"

What you are doing is isolating the objection. You don't want to work the trade allowance to death only to find out that the customer has no cash down or thinks the price of the car is too much. Remember the less negotiating the better the gross.

Customer: "No, everything else is ok; I just thought my trade was worth more."

DO NOT ASK THE CUSTOMER HOW MUCH THEY WANT!!

If you do they will throw a number at you so inflated that the manager will toss your deal out the door. In this example we allowed the customer $5000 for their trade. Let's see the right way to negotiate.

Salesperson: "I can appreciate that. What if I got my manager to give you $5100 for your trade?"

You asked a closing question and now be quiet and what for an answer.

Customer: "Oh no, I wouldn't trade for that."

Salesperson: "Ok, how about $5200?"

Customer: "I want $6000 for my trade!"

Salesperson: "Ok, so let me understand, if I can get you $6000 for your trade you will go ahead and buy my car now?"

Customer: "Yes."

Salesperson: "So let me write this that you want $6000 for your trade and I need your signature right here to present this to my manager."

Depending on your dealership you may get a deposit or the down payment at this time. I always encourage the salesperson to get the down payment at this point. Do not as two closing questions at once. Wait until the customer has signed the order and then you can ask for the down payment.

Salesperson: "Will the down payment be in cash or a check?"

Customer: "Check."

Salesperson: "Great, can you go ahead and make it out to (Dealership Name) and I will get everything going."

When a customer gives you money you will always have a buyer! Don't be afraid to ask for the money. It is another way of committing your customer to purchase.

Make sure you explain to your customer that you are going to present their offer to the manager and it should only take a few minutes. Now pick up all your paperwork and head to the manager.

The manager will now address your deal and ask you some questions. Make sure that you give the manager the down payment at this point. The manager will now make a written counter offer on the trade allowance for you to present to the customer. The good part about having the down payment is that the customer will not get up and run out of the dealership on a counter offer. Remember controlling the sale is key to success.

The managers states in writing that all they can give is $5500.

You go back to the customer and sit down. Remember to smile as you walk back from the manager. If you look like you have just been gutted, the customer is going to get very anxious and expect the worse before you ever get to them.

Salesperson: "Great news! I told my manager they we were apart on the trade and he went ahead and upped the trade to five thousand five hundred dollars! Isn't that great?

Closing question. Be quiet. Listen.

Customer: "I guess that will be ok, how long is this going to take?"

Now you shake the customer's hands and assure them that you will get them delivered as fast as possible and that it won't take that long. Collect driver's licenses, insurance cards, titles, registrations and any other required items and start putting together a deal package.

This method of closing will work on any objection that the customer will give you from the offer to purchase. Whether the customer has a trade or not, paying cash, trading two vehicles, whatever the case may be or you could be negotiating the purchase price or total drive out price or monthly payment. In any case always Identify, Isolate, Negotiate and Overcome the objection and never ask the customer what they want! It isn't how much you give, it is how many times you give that closes the customer.

Sometimes you might have to go back and forth to the manager a few times and you should always keep upbeat and smile. The customer will feel more at ease with the close if they feel you're not shook up about the deal. There are times when a customer won't close on an acceptable deal. At this time you need to realize you will need some help. The next step will explain how to increase your success in closing the deal with help from someone else.

11 TURN OVER IF NEEDED

So you have done everything and said everything you can think of and the customer still won't close. In reality the T.O. is used anytime that you cannot get the customer to do what you want them to. It doesn't matter what step you're on, if you can't get to the next step, get a T.O..

Setting up a T.O. is just as important as a T.O.. When you realize you are in trouble and need help the last thing you want to tell the customer is that you are going to get the manager. If you do that your customer will go on high alert and want to leave. The last thing that the customer wants to do is to talk with the manager. The better way is to put them at ease. A common word track that is successful is:

SALESPERSON: "He, I just had a great idea, hang on one second, I'll be right back."

Even if the customer watches you go to the manager, they are still wondering what the great idea you have is. In many cases the manager will take the T.O. and in some cases have a senior salesperson take the T.O.. In the either event just introduce the person that takes the T.O. to the customers and walk away out of hearing range. The reason for that is in many closes the real objection comes out on the T.O. but the customer wouldn't reveal it to you.

Don't pollute the T.O. person with what you think is wrong. Let that person find out the problem on their own. When I took a T.O. I would ask up to 3 questions.

How have you been treated since you're here?

The car you have picked, is it everything you want?

Why am I missing your business?

Sound familiar? It should by now. Three reasons customers don't buy from you.

They don't like you.

They don't like the vehicle.

They don't like the pricing.

99% of the time it will be one of those three problems. A good T.O. will sniff out the real objection and possibly save the deal.

You should never, I repeat, never feel as if you couldn't do your job when you ask for a T.O.. The only thing a T.O. can do for you is put money in your pocket.

Use all the tools available to you to become successful.

12 COMPLETION OF DEAL PAPERWORK

Your dealership has a procedure for creating a deal packet with what the Business Manager will need. Here is a sample list.

Deal Folder with cover sheet filled out.

Hand written sales order completed and signed by the customer and the manager.

Copy of all signers drivers license.

Copy if current insurance card and verification of new coverage on new vehicle.

Completed payoff authorization information form with 15 day payoff quote.

Actual title and registration to trade in.

Completed credit application on all signers.

Each dealership has internal forms that they require and are usually listed on a check list in the deal packet.

13 INTRODUCTION TO THE BUSINESS OFFICE

Finance office, financial services office, F&I, the box and the nicknames go on. This is where your customer signs all the paperwork involving the titling, registration, financing, insurance, and federal and state required paperwork. The person that works in the Business Office is usually paid by commission also. It is their job to sell the customer what is called "back-end" products such as extended warranties, gap insurance protection, credit life, credit disability. What does that mean to you? Some dealerships pay the salespeople spiffs on extended warranties and count "back-end" gross in to total gross for Salesperson of the Month award and bonus. More money, which is what it means to you. The customer is presented product and the Business Manager discloses the new payment and signs the customer to a contract.

NEVER TAKE YOUR CUSTOMER TO THE BUSINESS MANAGER WITHOUT BEING INSTRUCTED BY THE BUSINESS MANAGER.

Take the deal folder to the Business Manager and they will call you when they are ready. The Business Manager has to load the deal in to a computer and then print out all the required forms. While you're waiting for the Business Manager, stay with your customer and go over owner's manuals or other information about the vehicle. Do not go hang out on the patio with the other salespeople. You will alienate your customer by doing that.

Once you are asked to bring your customers to the Business Manager, take them to the office and have them sit down. Introduce the manager and the customers at this time.

Most Business Managers will like this introduction.

SALESPERSON: "Mr. and Mrs. Smith, this is my Business Manager (name) and it is their job to go over all the state and federal paper work and make sure it is correct. Also by the way, they are going to mention extended warranties, which I highly recommend. They will call me when you're finished and I should have your new car ready to go."

When they are finished in the business office do not ask the customer what their payments came out to be. Only thing that does is open a can of worms that you won't be able to close. Just congratulate them and thank them for their business.

By now you should have to get the car ready, the owner's manual, and the warranty books completed for delivery.

14 DELIVERY

Don't rush the delivery.

More so than any other step of the sale, this is the step that the customer always remembers. Make a lasting impression.

Most dealerships have a delivery area where the car is staged. While the customer was in with the Business Manager you should make sure the vehicle is clean and sparkling for delivery. You should have all the books ready and have the vehicle opened up. Once you have gone over the service schedule and warranty book, skim the owner's manual and encourage them to read it. It has a wealth of information.

Take the customer to the car and do another static presentation of the engine, trunk and cockpit areas. Go over all controls and switches. Make sure that all the lights are working with your customer participating.

Ask if you can help transfer belongings from the trade in. Make sure you check for garage door openers and stuff under the seats. Now that your customer is ready to leave you need to ask them if they have any questions and that they should feel free to call you if they have any questions later.

Watch as another one goes over the curb.

You just sold a car! Now what?

The best time to sell a car is right after you sold one!!!

You're on cloud 9 and your confidence is high. Go get another customer before it wears off.

15 FOLLOW UP

Follow up is not just calling a sold customer after the sale. Follow up is your future business. Many dealerships have found the importance of maintaining a data base of all customers that visit the dealership and have installed Customer Relationship Management (CRM) systems and personnel dedicated to that system. Being able to electronically recall, sort and print information on prospects, sold customers and referrals is a very large asset to a salesperson. It is important when inputting the customer's information in the system that you are very detailed in the information. When you access that information a year later the customer will appreciate that you remember them as well as their spouse and children's names as well what they purchased and traded in. That is what being a professional is all about. The down side is that if you leave that dealership, your files don't follow you. I have always suggested that along with the dealership files you keep your own record or backup copies of your database.

Now that you have sold a car you do need to start with follow up. You should contact a sold customer the next day, five days, two weeks and one month after the sale by phone. The purpose is to insure that everything is ok with the vehicle and to answer any questions they might have. You need to ask for referrals every time you speak to one of your sold customers. Here is a good word track for asking for referrals.

Salesperson: "By the way, can you give me the name and contact information on anyone you know that has mentioned that they may be in the market for a vehicle?"

When a customer refers someone to you and you sell that customer most dealerships send a "birddog" referral check. The referral amounts usually range from $50 to $250 depending on the dealership. Check with your management to find out the amount they send.

Most dealership CRM systems allow you to set up mail follow up and notify you of when to make phone contacts. I recommend that after the initial sold vehicle follow up that you send a contact letter every 6 months, on the customer's birthday, and on the holidays. You should phone contact the customer on the anniversary of the date of sale. Remember to always ask how they are and their family members are doing by name.

If your dealership is doing data-based marketing you will benefit from advertising dollars that the dealership spends. Usually when they mail to the data base about a sale or event, your customer is instructed to ask for you when they come in.

Quantify 12 sold per month and 3 sold referrals each month by 5 years. That is 900 sold customers. Now consider that if the national closing ratio is 10% you have a total of 8100 total prospects in your data base over the 5 year period. Some of the 8100 bought else ware, some couldn't purchase because of credit, and some just didn't buy. As an example, let's say only 40% of your database is useable for prospecting. That means that 3240 prospects can buy in the future.

Along with repeat and referral customers and your current prospect database you shouldn't have to go on the lot and catch an "up" to sell a car. The customers will be coming in and asking for you.

16 AFTER THE SALE

Selling vehicles can be great career however there are some pitfalls that will eventually run you out of the business. In every dealership there are the salespeople who constantly talk of gloom and doom, how there are no customers, or the inventory stinks, or the bonus plan isn't good enough. Stay away from these whiners. All they are going to do is mess up your attitude and work plan for the day.

Many of these whiners will disagree with this book. That is because they are ripe and rotten, not green and growing. My best advice is to only take advice from people who are doing better than you are. It does not make sense to take advice or listen to someone who is doing worse that you.

Make sure every day that you go to your dealership that you are the first one there. Go into the service area and ask if anybody would like a brochure. Talk to the customers in a friendly manner and give out your business card.

Have your day planned out with appointments, follow up and prospecting. The idea is either to be with a customer or be trying to find one to be with.

Keep up with product knowledge and your inventory. Nothing is more embarrassing then when a customer knows more about your products then you do.

Always hand out your business card to anyone that you are paying for something and tell them what you do. Most people will thank you and keep your card for future reference.

Whenever you lose a sale, ask the customer what you did wrong. The truth will make you better.

Don't blame others for when you lose a sale. You are in control of your own destiny.

CONCLUSION

I sincerely hope that this book will help you to reach your goals in life. Some of the best car people I know live by many of the suggestions and processes in this book. It is however up to you to decide whether or not you want to work smart or work hard. I have personally met salespeople in the business that never do follow up or care about future business. They think they can make a living off of the customers that walk on to the lot. That works for awhile, but in slow times it doesn't and those salespeople end up not selling any cars, whining about it and eventually quitting.

The steps to a sale have worked for decades in the same basic principles. You always can measure where you are in a sales process and if you need to revisit a step or get a T.O. You need to study and remember every step so when you are with a customer you know what you're doing. Practice with a spouse, friend, or in a mirror with a voice recorder so that you sound professional and confident when you're with a customer. You don't want to practice on a customer and blow the deal because of something you did or didn't do or something you did or didn't say. Too much effort goes into getting a customer in front of you and you better be on top of your game.

Selling is an attitude

Attitude comes from confidence

Confidence comes from training

Training comes from inspiration

INSPIRE YOURSELF

AND

INSPIRE SOMEONE ELSE

YOU AND THE WORLD WILL BE A BETTER PLACE

34933718R00044

Made in the USA
Lexington, KY
27 August 2014